THE
WILD
FOOD
GOURMET

THE
WILD
FOOD
GOURMET

Fresh and savory food from nature

Anne Gardon

FIREFLY BOOKS

A FIREFLY BOOK

Published by Firefly Books Ltd. 1998
Copyright © 1994 Les Editions de l'Homme
English text copyright © 1998 Firefly Books Ltd.
Photographs copyright © 1998 Anne Gardon

Cataloguing-in-Publication Data

Gardon, Anne
  The wild food gourmet

Translation of: La cuisine des champs.
Includes index.
ISBN 1-55209-242-9

1. Cookery (Wild foods). 2. Wild plants, Edible. 1. Title.

TX823.G36513 1998   641.6   C97-932795-4

Design: Gillian Tsintziras, The Brookview Group Inc.
Editor: Sarah Weber
Production: Denise Schon Books Inc.

Published in Canada in 1998
by Firefly Books Ltd.
3680 Victoria Park Avenue
Willowdale, Ontario
Canada M2H 3K1

Published in the United States in 1998
by Firefly Books (U.S.) Inc.
P.O. Box 1338, Ellicott Station
Buffalo, New York
USA 14205

Printed and bound in Canada by Friesens, Altona, Manitoba

Printed on acid-free paper

Visit Anne Gardon's web site at http://www.generation.net/~solstice

Dedication

I dedicate this book to nature lovers and gourmets alike.
And I wish to thank my friends who were brave enough
to test and taste my recipes.
Bon appétit to you all.

Contents

Introduction

Aboriginal people made extensive use of wild edibles, as food and as medicine. Our ancestors learned to identify them and included some in their diet. But how many of us know about wild edibles today? And how many of us could survive in the wilderness without food...store-bought food, that is!

Yet, nature provides us with a bounty of tender leaves, delicious berries, nutritious roots and tubers. Milkweed shoots as tender as asparagus, anise-flavored oxeye daisy leaves and buds, golden cattail pollen, fragrant mushrooms—a whole new range of tastes is at our fingertips.

Wild edibles bring a new twist to home cooking, cottage parties and camping trips. Much more than a free way to vary the menu, picking wild edibles is a passport to a secret world—full of wonders and bird songs—a world waiting for us at the edge of the city.

I have been eating wild edibles most of my life and I am not dead...yet! This may reassure the overly anxious.

As a child growing up in Provence, France, I used to follow my parents on their quest for wild asparagus, edible weeds, berries and mushrooms. When I came to Canada, I discovered a totally different and fascinating vegetation.

But my foray into Mother Nature's larder really started when I took up backpacking. I would disappear into the woods for days on end, loaded with cameras, binoculars, nature books and little room for food. Turning to my hostess for sustenance seemed the logical solution. So I added more books to my load—among them *Stalking the Wild Asparagus* by Euell Gibbons—and started harvesting and eating wild edibles. Much to my surprise, what I had considered "survival food" turned out to be delicious.

I don't go backpacking much anymore. Having moved to the country, my need for fresh air and escape is now satisfied. I have also become passionate about gardening, which occupies much of my time from spring to fall. But that doesn't mean I have "civilized" my eating habits. On the contrary, I have extended my foraging, as there are many more wild edibles in meadows and around country homes than along hiking trails.

Trading the campfire for the kitchen stove has also allowed me to refine my "wild recipes" and to present nature's offerings in the best possible light.

Cooking with wild edibles is a gratifying experience from start to finish...well almost!

First there is the joy of walking through fragrant fields or mossy under-woods, a wonderful pastime to share with children.

Then, there is the task of cleaning the harvest, especially tedious in the case of dandelions that have to be washed several times. But the effort is little to pay for a scrumptious dandelion leaf salad, chock-full of vitamins and minerals.

Just as tasty as "regular" food, wild edibles can also be as nutritious, which makes them a welcome addition to any diet.

Many wild plants are edible but not all are interesting from a culinary standpoint. Some are tough or bitter; others demand long preparation or have little taste. For this book, I have chosen my favorite plants, full of flavor, easy to identify and pick and, of course, plants that are not threatened by extinction.

My recipes are easy, economical, healthy and quick to prepare. I have also combined food gathered in the wild with fresh produce from the market to capture the seasonal flavors.

I do not believe I could survive just on wild edibles. Gnawing on birch bark or chewing evergreen buds during the winter months doesn't exactly appeal to me. But drop me off in the wilderness in summer and you will make me very happy...gastronomically speaking.

A Few Words on Foraging

It is imperative that you learn to identify edible plants before starting on any culinary experiment, especially when mushrooms or poisonous plants are concerned. Do not use any plant that you cannot identify positively. Many good identification guides are available to help you. In my opinion it is easier to identify plants from pictures—if they are good, of course—than from drawings. I like the convenience of pocket-size books as you can easily carry them when foraging.

On almost all public land, gathering wild edibles or removing plants is illegal and should not be done. Go foraging only on private property and only with the owner's permission. Very rarely will it be refused.

Limit your picking to what you can eat or prepare the same day. Always leave enough to insure the plant's survival and do not damage the surrounding vegetation.

Leaves are picked when young and tender; flowers are gathered as soon as they open. Different species of mushrooms are available at different times, from early spring to late fall. Cut mushrooms with a sharp knife and use paper bags to carry and store them.

Preserving

Wild edibles are at their best when fresh. But that doesn't mean part of the harvest cannot be preserved for later use.

Herbs and mushrooms can be dried. Lamb's quarters, cattail pollen, fiddleheads, milkweed flower buds and a few species of mushrooms can be frozen. Berries make wonderful jams and jellies.

Drying

Herbs that are to be dried should be picked early in the morning as soon as the dew is off the plants, or in the evening. Avoid humid or rainy days.

Pick off yellowing or insect-nibbled parts. Remove the leaves from the branches and spread the leaves on a screen. Another method is to tie the leafy branches into a bundle and hang it up to dry. This is especially useful for stinging nettle. An attic, a shady porch or a shed—in fact any place that is hot and dry with no direct sun—is a good place to dry herbs.

To dry mushrooms, clean them and cut meaty caps into slices about 1/8 to 1/4 inch (4 to 6 mm) thick, separate coral fungus (*Ramaria*) into flowerettes, or leave fairy ring mushrooms whole. Spread mushrooms on a screen and dry in a hot, shady spot until they become leathery or brittle.

Keep dried herbs and mushrooms in clean, dry glass jars in a cupboard or dark place, never in the sun.

Freezing

One method of freezing herbs such as mint and yarrow is to chop them finely, pack them into ice cube trays and cover them with water. Once they have frozen solid, store the cubes in a plastic bag. Do not forget to label the bag. To make herbal tea, drop a cube into the teapot, cover with boiling water and let steep a few minutes.

Steam lamb's quarters and blanch fiddle-heads and cattail shoots 1 minute before freezing.

Mushrooms such as boletes and chanterelles are frozen raw, either whole or in chunks depending on their size. Clean the mushrooms, spread them on a tray and freeze. Store in a plastic bag or container.

Berries can be frozen using two methods.

Open freezing

This method keeps individual pieces separate so they do not freeze in a solid mass. Clean berries, spread them on a baking sheet or a tray and freeze. Pack them in bags or containers. Frozen berries keep 6 months.

Sugar packing

This method is for freezing whole, sliced or crushed fruits. In a rigid container, alternate layers of fruit and sugar, using about 1 cup (250 mL) of sugar for every 2 pounds (1 kg) of fruit. Leave 1-1/8 inches (3 cm) of headroom before sealing the container.

Juices and Syrups

Concentrated fruit juices are used to make jellies, coulis (see page142) or cold drinks.

Concentrate

To preserve the flavor of the berries, it is best to use a pressure cooker. Put fruit in the pot; cover hard fruits such as wild apples with water; add just a little water to soft fruits or berries. Raise the pressure over high heat until steam comes out of the vent with a steady hissing noise. Remove immediately from heat and cool the sides of the cooker under cold running water to bring the pressure down.

When using a regular pot, boil fruits until tender, about 5 minutes for soft flesh fruits and 15 to 20 minutes for hard fruits. Strain the fruit in a jelly bag or a fine sieve overnight. Keep the pulp from apples to make Apple Butter (see page 168).

Syrup

Slowly bring fruit concentrate to a boil, adding sugar until desired sweetness is reached. Boil 1 minute, strain and pour into sterilized bottles or jars. Keep in the fridge or a cool place. Use as is over ice cream, or as a coulis to coat a serving plate for a dessert. Thickened with unflavored gelatin, fruit syrups make a delicious glazing for cakes. Dilute with water for a refreshing drink in place of commercial juice.

Wild Greens and Flowers

I live south of Montreal in a region blessed with a microclimate. My house is surrounded by meadows and woodlands where I do most of my foraging. But, for convenience, I have also transplanted several wild edibles to my garden, and I pamper the ones that establish themselves naturally, such as sheep sorrel, evening primrose, and winter cress.

For me, there is no such thing as a bad weed. I always find use for them, whether to enrich the compost pile, to eat or to feed to the chickens. Wild plants can be also very decorative, as we are beginning to find out in the current trend for natural gardens.

My Favorite Wild Greens and Flowers

Fiddleheads

Oxeye daisy

Dandelion

Common chickweed

Orpine

Milkweed

Lamb's quarters

Cattail

Sheep sorrel

Mint

Jewelweed

Stinging nettle

Wild mustard

Winter cress

Fiddleheads

Fiddleheads (ostrich fern)
Matteuccia struthiopteris

What we call fiddleheads are the young fronds of the ostrich fern. They appear in May along streambanks, in open woods and at the edge of swamps, from Canada to the north of Virginia.

Fiddleheads must be picked before they unfurl, when they are about three to five inches (a few centimeters) high. Always leave a few fronds to insure the plant's survival.

To clean them, place fiddleheads in an apron attached around your waist and shake the apron vigorously in the open air. The brown, papery scales of the fiddleheads will fly to the wind. Wash off the rest under running water.

Cook fiddleheads in boiling water for 2 to 3 minutes or steam them until tender.

Oxeye daisy
Chrysanthemum leucanthemum

The young, tender leaves of this plant have a sweet aniseed taste. Buds can be pickled like capers or added to tomato sauce (blanch 1 minute beforehand), and the dried flowers make a delicious tea (see page 157).

Daisies belong to the Chrysanthemum family and are found throughout North America. They prefer poor, dry soil and open fields.

Dandelion

Common chickweed

Dandelion
Taraxacum officinale

Trees have not yet leafed when dandelions are already showing their fuzzy heads. This hated weed is in fact the best thing nature can give us in spring. Full of vitamins and minerals—2 ounces (60 g) of dandelion leaves provide the recommended daily dose of vitamin A and half the daily dose of vitamin C—dandelion helps restore our failing health after the winter. But pick it early, before the flowering bud shows its head and the leaves become bitter.

A salad, seasoned with olive oil, lemon juice and a pinch of salt, is the best and easiest way to savor dandelion leaves. For fresh greens in the winter months, force dandelion (or chicory) roots indoors (see page 35).

Common chickweed
Stellaria media

Present throughout the northern hemisphere, chickweed grows around habitations and in fields, from early spring to the last frost. Delicious in salads, the leaves can also be cooked.

Orpine

Milkweed

Lamb's quarters

Orpine
Sedum purpureum

Rich in vitamin C, orpine leaves are crunchy and refreshing. Pick top leaves and add them to salads. The leaves can also be pickled or cooked.

Milkweed
Asclepias syriaca

This tall perennial grows freely in fields left fallow. Pink flower clusters bloom in July, attracting many butterflies. It is the only food source for the monarch butterfly larva, which, having fed on the noxious leaves, becomes unpalatable to birds. It is not unusual to see monarch cocoons hanging from milkweed leaves.

Like cattail, milkweed is edible at various stages. In spring, the young shoots are eaten like asparagus and taste not unlike that vegetable. Similar to broccoli in taste and look, flower buds are picked in June, and the young fruits are gathered in July.

Milkweed is very rich in vitamin C, but most of it is lost during cooking, however, as all parts of the plant must be boiled in two or three changes of water to eliminate the bitter, milky sap. Plunge milkweed into boiling water, cook 1 minute, drain and repeat.

Lamb's quarters
Chenopodium album

This annual belongs to the spinach and beet family. For a long time, lamb's quarters ended up on my compost pile. Then I found out I was throwing away an excellent source of vitamin C and iron. Now, lamb's quarters grows freely at the edge of my garden. Harvest runs from spring to the middle of summer. Though it can be eaten raw, I prefer it lightly steamed.

Rinse and, without shaking, throw the leaves in a saucepan. Cook at medium heat till wilted. Drain and press with a wooden spoon to extract all the liquid.

Lamb's quarters is often dusted with a white substance. This is normal and should not worry you. Recipes calling for spinach—those called florentine—are suitable for lamb's quarters. Spinach can likewise be substituted for lamb's quarters in the recipes in this book.

Cattail

Typha angustifolia and *Typha latifolia*

One of the most important plants of our environment, cattails prevent erosion of lakeshores and rivers and help clean polluted waters. These plants also provide shelter and food for birds, muskrats and many other animals.

Cattails are precious wild edibles, a real "supermarket" plant. In spring, the young, tender shoots are eaten like—and are reminiscent of—leeks. In June, the male cattail spikes can be picked, cooked in boiling water and eaten like corn on the cob. The male part is the upper, narrower section of the cattail spike. When emerging, both male and female parts are wrapped in a green membrane. It is at this stage that the male part must be picked. Break it off where it meets the lower section. The male spike blooms rapidly, becoming soft and covered with a bright yellow powdery pollen that makes a light flour, rich in taste and color. Check your cattail patch regularly, as the flowering season is very short, two weeks at the most. To collect cattail pollen, bend the spike into a large paper bag and shake. It sounds like an awfully tedious process, but I bet you can harvest a pound or two in an hour. Cattail pollen keeps well for up to a year in the freezer.

Cattail

Sheep sorrel

Mint

Sheep sorrel
Rumex acetosella

This tiny plant with *fleur de lys* leaves has digestive and diuretic properties. Sheep sorrel runs wild under my raspberry canes. A handful is enough to add zing to any salad.

Sheep sorrel contains oxalates. If eaten in excess, it can cause calcium deficiencies and kidney troubles. But, let's not panic! Oxalates are also present in beets, spinach and other vegetables.

Sheep sorrel grows in meadows, gardens and along country roads, from June till September. It is found all over the North American continent, except in the high Arctic.

Mint
Mentha

There are three main varieties of mint: spearmint (*Mentha spicata*), peppermint (*M. piperita*) and American mint (*M. canadensis*). All grow in wetlands, along rivers and on lakeshores. I discovered a fabulous patch in a ditch while harvesting cattail pollen. Antiseptic and analgesic, mint tea helps digestion and stimulates the liver. Mint baths are refreshing and calm sunburns.

Jewelweed

Winter cress

There are other wild edibles that I use occasionally, when they are in season or particularly abundant.

Jewelweed
Impatiens pallida and *Impatiens capensis*

There are two varieties of impatiens (also called touch-me-not), one with pale yellow flowers and one with orange spotted blossoms, both of which have an orchid like appearance. They grow on tall stems in wet, shady places, from Canada south to Florida. Spring shoots make a nice, refreshing addition to salads. The juice of crushed stems and leaves soothes the sting of nettles and is said to prevent the rash from poison ivy.

Stinging nettle
Urtica spp.

Nettles are forbidding and rather ugly. The young shoots of stinging nettle can be picked in spring when they are 2 to 8 inches (5 to 20 centimeters) high and eaten fresh like spinach or added to soups and stews.

Wild mustard
Brassica kaber

Fields of wild mustard are bright yellow in summer and a joy for the eye, but for farmers, this plant is one of the most invasive weeds. Seeds are active for up to 15 years and make the plant almost impossible to get rid of. For us "wild pickers" though, the young tender leaves are a real treat—tangy, crunchy and full of vitamins and minerals—a nice addition to a salad. Wild mustard is found throughout North America.

Winter cress
Barbareas vulgaris

Similar to wild mustard, winter cress has darker leaves that are delicious in salads. But they must be picked very early in spring as they become bitter quickly. Winter cress blooms in spring. The yellow flowers can be added to salads but do not include the very bitter upper leaves.

The plant is found in moist waste grounds in the eastern part of the continent.

Wild Greens and Flowers in the Garden

Wildflowers and plants play a great role in my garden. Masses of yarrow border the vegetable garden where they attract insects. I use the leaves to make a liquid fertilizer and to make a poultice whenever I am stung by insects. Violets brighten my shade garden. Mint mingles with cattails around the pond and orpine competes with daylilies for space.

Sturdy, usually insect free and disease resistant, wild plants are easy to grow if the natural conditions they require are respected. Some like it dry; some like it wet! Some need acid soil; others grow only on mountain tops or by the seashore. The laws of nature are not rigid, though. For several years, I grew a clump of Scotch lovage brought back from Pointe-des-Monts, north of Baie-Comeau in Quebec. I had my doubts about its survival as I had transplanted it from a saline environment to totally different climatic conditions. Far from being homesick, my Scotch lovage adapted very well. Sadly, it died at the feet of a clumsy contractor doing repairs, but it taught me that you can fool nature some of the time. You just have to experiment.

Black Raspberries

Blackberry
Rubus spp.

Red and black raspberries as well as blackberries are part of the Rubus family. In the fall, year-old canes bend naturally toward the earth where they take root by the tip. You can bury the end of several canes in a pot full of soil, secure them in place with wire or a stone and wait until spring to transplant the new shoots. Or you can dig out small clumps of young canes, being careful to keep a good chunk of earth around the roots. Blackberries need light, well-drained soil rich in organic matter. If necessary, add peat moss and compost. Like raspberries, blackberries grow on canes that are two years old. After producing fruit, the canes die and should be pruned off at ground level. New canes will grow to replace them.

Dandelion
Taraxacum officinale

Dandelion roots can be forced indoors with the same method that is used for Belgian endive. In the fall, dig out the plants without damaging the roots. Plant in a deep container filled with soil or sand. Cover with a sheet of black plastic and keep in a cool, dark place, ideally a cold cellar. In the deep of winter, when your vitamin count is getting low, start uncovering the container. Harvest the young, white shoots as needed for crispy, invigorating salads. Chicory roots (*Chichorium intybus*) can also be forced and the leaves used in the same way as dandelion.

Gooseberries and Currants
Ribes spp.

There are approximately 120 species of these fruit-bearing bushes. They grow at the edge of wooded areas. Some cultivated varieties—black currant and gooseberry—escaped from gardens and have naturalized. For the best decorative effect, choose the American black currant (*R. americanum*), a handsome bush with veined bark and a multitude of tiny yellow flowers that appear in spring. Dig out young plants in spring, keeping a good clump of earth around the roots. Plant in rich soil in a shady spot. Wild black currant can carry a disease that affects white pines, so choose healthy specimens.

Mint (spearmint, peppermint)
Mentha spp.

Wild mint grows just as easily as cultivated mint. Moist soil and a shaded spot are preferable though mint will adapt to most situations. In spring, lift the creeping stems, divide them, keeping a joint in every piece, and transplant them to a shallow trench. Water often, especially when recently transplanted. As mint is invasive, choose an area where it can run freely, or grow it in containers.

Orpine (live-forever)
Sedum purpureum

This succulent perennial is astonishingly tough, thus the name "live-forever." It is said that a dry branch of this species will root if planted. Orpine grows in fields, along country roads and at the edge of woodlands, in dry and wet areas, in full sun or in the shade. Dig out the whole plant or take cuttings and plant them directly in the soil. Cover with mulch and water regularly until the pieces have taken root.

Riverbank grape
Vitis riparia

Wild grape seeds germinate quickly but the plant takes several years to reach maturity and produce fruits. So it is better to propagate by cutting or layering. Instructions for layering are available in many gardening books.

Propagation by cuttings is best done in the fall. Choose a young, healthy branch and cut it into several pieces, each with at least four nodes. Bury the cuttings half way in light soil (one-third each of black earth, sand or vermiculite, and peat moss). Cover with a plastic bag and put in a cool place like a garage or a basement (40 to 50°F/5 to 10°C). Keep the soil moist. In spring, bring the cuttings out of their dormancy by moving them gradually to warmer quarters over a one-week period. Within a few weeks, buds should appear. Plant when the soil has warmed up and all danger of frost has passed.

Sheep sorrel
Rumex acetosella

Once established, this small perennial will provide tender leaves for several years. Pick seeds in July and sow in a corner of the garden as it can become invasive. Sheep sorrel propagates itself by seeds but also by underground runners.

Stinging nettle
Urtica spp.

Stinging nettle is a compost activator. Add a few handfuls of chopped fresh leaves to the compost pile. It also makes a rich organic fertilizer. Harvest leaves when young. Put stinging nettle leaves (you may also add yarrow, tansy, valerian and comfrey leaves) in a big garbage bin. Cover with water and steep for 2 weeks. Dilute 1:20 for watering ornamental plants and vegetables or 1:10 for spraying on leaves. Use immediately as it does not keep.

To pick stinging nettle, wear gloves and long sleeves as the stalks and leaves are covered with stinging hairs.

Violet
Viola spp.

In the symbolism of flowers, the violet means modesty and faithfulness. And indeed, violets are faithful as they will come back year after year if you plant them in your garden. Dig plants out in spring, keeping a good clump of earth around the roots. Transplant to a shaded, moist spot. Violets produce seed pods that mature in July. Pick and seed immediately in cool, moist soil. Leaves and flowers are edible, and both are rich in vitamins. Harvest when young.

Oxeye daisy
Chrysanthemum leucanthemum

This rustic perennial can easily be transplanted to the garden so that tender young shoots will always be at hand. But, beware! Wild daisies reseed themselves freely and can become invasive. Choose a secluded spot or cut blooms as they fade.

Yarrow
Achillea millefolium

Yarrow is a useful perennial to have in the garden because the leaves make a liquid fertilizer and insecticide. Dig out plants in spring. Transplant to a sunny location with light soil. Leave ample space between plants as they spread quickly.

Cinnamon fern

Sunny Salad

Makes 4 servings

As an appetizer or a side dish, this light salad will bring sunshine to your meal.

Ingredients

4 cups (1 L) fiddleheads
4 oranges
4 Belgian endives
olive oil
salt
pepper

Method

1. Clean and cook fiddleheads (see below). Cool.
2. With a sharp knife, peel oranges removing all white part. Cut oranges in thick slices, then in quarters, removing pits at the same time. Cut endives crosswise into rounds.
3. Arrange fiddleheads, oranges and endives in a serving bowl. Season with olive oil, salt and pepper. Serve cold.

Fiddleheads are sold commercially, fresh in spring or frozen at any time of year. Cook fiddleheads in boiling water for 2 to 3 minutes, or steam them until tender. Drain.

Cinnamon Fern: When gathering fiddleheads, be careful not to pick Cinnamon fern, which may cause upset stomach. Both ferns have similar heads, though those of Cinnamon fern are covered with a pale fuzz, either white or creamy in color.

Maritime Fiddleheads

Makes 4 servings

This colorful dish is my homage to Californian cuisine, which I love for its bold colors and interesting mix of flavors.

Ingredients
1 red bell pepper
1 yellow bell pepper
1 large red onion
1/2 cup (125 mL) olive oil
1/2 cup (125 mL) balsamic vinegar
salt
pepper
4 cups (1 L) fiddleheads*
16 large shrimp**
1 package (16 oz/454 g) angel hair noodles

Method
1. Cut peppers and half the onion in big chunks. Mince rest of the onion. Combine oil, vinegar, minced onion, salt and pepper and mix well.
2. Pour oil mixture over peppers and onion pieces and let marinate 1 hour. In the meantime, cook fiddleheads (see page 39).
3. Clean and devein shrimp. Sauté lightly in oil until pink (2 minutes). Remove from pan and keep warm.
4. Drain vegetables, reserving marinade. Sauté vegetables 2 minutes in oil. Add fiddleheads and shrimp, cover and simmer a few minutes.
5. At the same time in separate pans, reduce marinade by half over high heat, and cook noodles according to directions on package.
6. Arrange vegetables and shrimp over noodles. Pour marinade over and serve immediately.

*Broccoli can be substituted.

**Chicken or pork in cubes can be substituted.

Fiddleheads Sarah Chang

Makes 4 appetizer servings

I am a great admirer of Canadian violinist Sarah Chang, and I dedicate this recipe with Asian flavors to her.

Ingredients

4 cups (1 L) fiddleheads

Dressing
4 tbsp (60 mL) roasted sesame seeds
4 tbsp (60 mL) soy sauce
2 tbsp (30 mL) water
1 tbsp (15 mL) sesame oil
1 tbsp (15 mL) vegetable oil
1 tbsp (15 mL) lemon juice
1 tsp (5 mL) fresh ginger juice (see below)
1 tsp (5 mL) sugar

Method

1. Clean and cook fiddleheads (see page 39).
2. Grind sesame seeds in a mortar. Combine all ingredients of the dressing and mix well. Pour over fiddleheads and serve warm or cold.

Fresh ginger juice is made by pressing a piece of ginger root in a garlic press.

Woodsy Fiddleheads

Makes 4 servings

Acadians used fiddleheads to cure high blood pressure.

Ingredients
4 cups (1 L) fiddleheads
1 large onion
2 cups (500 mL) white mushrooms*
3 tbsp (45 mL) butter
1/2 cup (125 mL) pine nuts
thyme
marjoram
salt
pepper
cooked wild rice

Method
1. Clean and cook fiddleheads (see page 39).
2. Slice onion and, if mushrooms are large, cut them into quarters. Sauté onion lightly in butter, 2 minutes. Add mushrooms and cook another 2 minutes, at medium heat.
3. Add fiddleheads and pine nuts. Season with herbs, salt and pepper. Cover and simmer 5 minutes.
4. Serve on a bed of wild rice.

*In season, wild mushrooms such as meadow mushrooms, chanterelles, shaggy manes or russulas can be substituted.

Mesclun

Makes 4 servings

This refreshing salad is a good accompaniment for Yarrow-flavored Goat Cheese (see page 98).

Ingredients
2 cups (500 mL) chickweed
1 cup (250 mL) orpine
1 cup (250 mL) parsley
1 cup (250 mL) watercress
1 cup (250 mL) chervil (optional)

Vinaigrette
1/4 cup (60 mL) olive oil
2 tbsp (30 mL) lemon juice
2 tsp (10 mL) prepared hot mustard
salt
pepper

Method
1. Combine salad greens.
2. Combine ingredients of the vinaigrette. Mix well. Pour over salad and toss.

Mesclun means mixed salad in the French dialect of Nice. Traditionally, mesclun is a combination of various plants and herbs from Provence, such as dandelion, arugula, chicory, and chervil.

Chicken Livers and Dandelion Salad

Makes 4 servings

This is a "wild" take on the French classic, warm chicory salad. The mild taste of chicken liver is perked up by the sharp flavor of dandelion leaves.

Ingredients

4 handfuls dandelion leaves
4 chicken livers
4 tbsp (60 mL) vegetable oil
2 onions, minced
salt
pepper
croutons
2 tbsp (30 mL) balsamic vinegar

Method

1. Clean dandelion leaves thoroughly and arrange on serving plates.
2. Cut each liver into 3 or 4 pieces.
3. In a pan, heat oil and cook onions 2 minutes. Add livers and sauté rapidly until firm but still pink inside. Season with salt and pepper.
4. Arrange livers on dandelion leaves. Garnish with croutons.
5. Deglaze pan with balsamic vinegar. Pour sauce over livers and serve warm.

Rich in iron, dandelion is tonic and digestive, diuretic and generally stimulating to the system. Just what our winter weary bodies need.

Dandelion Salad

Makes 4 servings

Early spring is the time to pick the greens for this delicious and nutritious salad.

Ingredients

4 cups (1 L) dandelion leaves
4 slices bacon
2 eggs

Dressing
1 tsp (5 mL) prepared hot mustard
2 tbsp (30 mL) balsamic vinegar
1/4 cup (60 mL) olive oil
salt
pepper
croutons

Method

1. Clean dandelion leaves thoroughly.
2. Cook bacon until crisp. Drain on paper towels, then crumble.
3. Poach eggs 3 minutes in boiling water. Drain.
4. Combine mustard with vinegar; add oil while beating. Season with salt and pepper.
5. Arrange dandelion leaves on serving plates. Garnish with croutons and bacon chips. Pour dressing over and top with poached egg.

Poached egg: Combine 2 cups (500 mL) water and 2 tbsp (30 mL) white vinegar. Bring to a boil. Break egg into a cup. Swirl a spoon in the water to create a whirlpool effect. Drop egg delicately in the middle. It will keep its shape.

Spring Salad

Makes 4 servings

Delicious and especially pretty, this salad will surprise many a friend.

Ingredients

2 cups (500 mL) oxeye daisy sprigs
2 cups (500 mL) dandelion leaves
1 cup (250 mL) violet leaves and flowers
1 cup (250 mL) sheep sorrel

Dressing
1/2 cup (125 mL) olive oil
3 tbsp (45 mL) lemon juice
1 tbsp (15 mL) prepared hot mustard
3 tbsp (45 mL) capers, minced (optional)
salt
pepper

Method

1. Combine salad greens and flowers.
2. Combine oil, lemon juice and mustard. Mix well. Add capers, salt and pepper to taste.
3. Pour dressing over salad, toss and serve.

The violet was the flower emblem of Napoleon Bonaparte's supporters. There are many varieties of violet, with blue, white, mauve or yellow flowers.

Daisy Tabouleh

Makes 4 servings

Bursting with vitamins, this salad makes an ideal accompaniment for Lamb and Mint Rolls (see page 82). When marinated in vinegar, oxeye daisy flower buds can be used to replace capers.

Ingredients
1-1/2 cups (375 mL) water
1 cup (250 mL) bulgur
1 small cucumber
1 ripe tomato
2 cups (500 mL) oxeye daisy leaves, chopped
1 cup (250 mL) parsley, chopped
several mint leaves, chopped (optional)
olive oil
lemon juice
salt
pepper

Method
1. Boil water with a pinch of salt. Add bulgur, cover and cook over very low heat until tender, about 10 minutes.
2. Rinse bulgur under cold running water and drain.
3. Peel cucumber. Dice cucumber and tomato. Add to bulgur, daisies, parsley and mint.
4. Drizzle with olive oil and lemon juice. Season with salt and pepper. Chill at least 2 hours before serving.

Milkweed Flower Buds in Vinaigrette

Makes 4 appetizer servings

Very nutritious, this warm salad can be served as an appetizer or as the main dish of a light lunch.

Ingredients

3 cups (750 mL) milkweed flower buds*
4 to 6 spring potatoes
1 green onion
tarragon sprig (optional)

Dressing

2 tbsp (30 mL) lemon juice or vinegar
1 tsp (5 mL) prepared hot mustard
1/4 cup (60 mL) olive oil
salt
pepper

Method

1. Cook milkweed flower buds in boiling water for 1 minute. Drain and repeat (see page 25). Cook potatoes separately, drain and cube. Mince onion and tarragon and add to milkweed and potatoes.
2. Mix lemon juice and mustard. Beat in oil gradually. Add salt and pepper to taste. Pour dressing over salad, toss and serve warm.

*Broccoli can be substituted.

Milkweed is also called butterfly weed, as it is much appreciated by butterflies and many other insects. Its Latin name, Asclepias, comes from Aesculapius, Greek god of medicine and healing. In the old days, milkweed shoots were sold for two cents a bunch in Montreal markets.

Lamb's Quarters Lasagne

Makes 4 servings

A nice dandelion salad with bacon bits and a fine Chianti to accompany this lasagne, and you'll think you are in Italy.

Ingredients

2 cups (500 mL) cooked lamb's quarters, chopped (see page 57)
2 cups (500 mL) cooked spinach or rapini*
1 medium onion
oil
2 cups (500 mL) cottage or ricotta cheese
1 cup (250 mL) grated Cheddar cheese
salt
pepper
2 cups (500 mL) tomato sauce
lasagna sheets (oven ready)

Method

1. Preheat oven to 350°F (180°C).
2. Sauté onion in a small amount of oil until transparent.
3. Combine lamb's quarters and spinach or rapini with onion, cheese, salt and pepper.
4. Pour some tomato sauce in bottom of ovenproof dish. Spread a layer of lasagne, cover with filling. Repeat until all ingredients are used. Finish with tomato sauce. Sprinkle with grated cheese and bake 35 to 40 minutes.

*Rapini, also called rapi or Italian broccoli, is a spinachlike plant rich in calcium, iron and vitamins. It is available in Italian and Asian markets.

The same filling can be used to stuff cannelloni.

Lamb's Quarters Flan

Makes 4 servings (microwave)

Your family snubs vegetables? Serve them this delicious flan and they will ask for more.

Ingredients
2 cups (500 mL) cooked lamb's quarters, chopped (see page 57)
1/4 cup (60 mL) butter
3 tbsp (45 mL) flour
salt
pepper
1 cup (250 mL) milk
3 eggs

Method
1. Preheat oven to 375°F (190°C).
2. Prepare a thick white sauce: Melt butter over low heat. Stir in flour, salt and pepper. Cook, stirring, for 3 minutes, then whisk in milk. Continue cooking and stirring until smooth and fully thickened, about 5 minutes. Combine with lamb's quarters. Beat in eggs, one at a time. Season to taste.
3. Pour mixture into buttered small ovenproof dishes (ramekins) or tartlet pans. Place ramekins in a large ovenproof dish containing 3/4 inch (2 cm) warm water and bake 15 minutes. Or cook in microwave oven, 5 minutes at High.
4. Unmold and serve with meat or fish.

Lamb's quarters contains more iron than any other green leafy vegetable except parsley, as well as vitamin C and some vitamin A. Because lamb's quarters contains oxalates that interfere with calcium absorption, eating great amounts of it may lead to a calcium deficiency. But consumed in moderate quantities, lamb's quarters is depurative, emollient and laxative.

Lamb's Quarters Quiche

Makes 4 to 6 servings

This wild version of the classic spinach quiche is a good source of iron and vitamins.

Ingredients

Pie pastry
2 cups (500 mL) flour
1/3 cup (80 mL) butter
1/3 cup (80 mL) shortening
cold water

Filling
2 cups (500 mL) cooked lamb's quarters, chopped (see page 57)
3 eggs
1 cup (250 mL) cottage cheese
pinch nutmeg
salt
pepper

Method

1. Preheat oven to 375°F (190°C).
2. Sift flour. Cut or rub in butter and shortening until mixture resembles bread crumbs. Add enough cold water to form a soft but not sticky dough. Wrap and chill 15 minutes.
3. Roll out dough and line pie dish.
4. Combine lamb's quarters with eggs and cottage cheese. Season with nutmeg, salt and pepper and mix well. Pour filling into pie pastry and bake 35 to 40 minutes.

Cheesy Ravioli

Makes 4 servings

What to do on a rainy weekend? Make ravioli and freeze them for sunnier or busier days.

Ingredients

Pasta dough
1-1/2 cups (375 mL) flour
2 eggs
4 tbsp (60 mL) oil
salt
cold water

Filling
1 cup (250 mL) cooked lamb's quarters, chopped (see page 57)
1/2 cup (125 mL) cream cheese
1/2 cup (125 mL) grated Parmesan

Parmesan sauce
2 tbsp (30 mL) butter
1 tbsp (15 mL) flour
1 cup (250 mL) milk
1 cup (250 mL) grated Parmesan

Method

1. Combine flour, eggs, oil and a pinch of salt. Add enough cold water to form a soft dough. Wrap and chill 1 hour.
2. Combine lamb's quarters with cream cheese and Parmesan.
3. Roll out pasta dough to desired thickness. Place small amount of filling at regular intervals. Cover with another sheet of dough. Press to eliminate air bubbles and cut into ravioli.
4. Prepare a white sauce: Melt butter over low heat. Stir in flour. Cook, stirring, for 3 minutes, then whisk in milk. Continue cooking and stirring until smooth and fully thickened, about 5 minutes. Add Parmesan. Mix well. Dilute with milk if too thick.
5. Cook ravioli 1 to 2 minutes in boiling water. Serve with Parmesan sauce.

Curried Cattail Soup

Makes 4 servings

Curry powder is an essential element of Indian cuisine and there are as many variations as there are households in India.

Ingredients

3 tbsp (45 mL) butter
1 onion, minced
1 tbsp (15 mL) curry powder
3 tbsp (45 mL) flour
2-1/2 cups (625 mL) chicken stock
12 cattail shoots, minced*
salt
pepper

Method

1. In a saucepan, melt butter and cook onion over medium heat until soft.
2. Sprinkle with curry powder and flour and cook 2 minutes, stirring.
3. Add chicken stock and cattails. Bring to a boil, reduce heat and simmer 15 minutes.
4. Add salt and pepper to taste. Serve hot.

*Leeks can be substituted.

To pick cattails, place your feet on either side of the shoot. Grasp the base of the shoot with both hands and pull up. Remove the green top leaving 6 to 8 inches (15 to 20 cm) of the white part of the shoot. Peel two or more layers of leaves to keep only the white tender part.

Cattail Shoots with Gribiche Sauce

Makes 4 servings

Gribiche sauce is an egg emulsion, like mayonnaise, but is made with hard-boiled egg.

Ingredients

20 cattail shoots

Gribiche sauce
1 hard-boiled egg
1 cup (250 mL) olive oil
2 tbsp (30 mL) lemon juice
2 tbsp (30 mL) capers, chopped
1 tbsp (15 mL) chopped chives
salt
pepper

Method

1. Boil cattails 3 to 5 minutes. Drain and cool.
2. Mash the cooked egg yolk and whisk in the oil slowly. Chop egg white.
3. To yolk mixture add lemon juice, capers, chopped egg white, salt and pepper.
4. Arrange shoots on serving plates. Pour sauce over and sprinkle with chives.
5. The same sauce can be used with boiled cattail spikes.

There are two types of cattails, those with thin leaves and those with broad leaves. Both are edible, but the broadleaved variety is meatier.

Cattail and Ham Rolls

One roll is a quick lunch, two rolls make an impromptu supper, but three rolls are pure gourmandise.

Ingredients
Per roll
3 cattail shoots
1 slice Black Forest ham
1 slice Gruyère or Jarlsberg cheese
prepared hot mustard
white wine

Method
1. Preheat oven to 375°F (190°C).
2. Cook shoots 3 to 5 minutes in boiling water.
3. Lay ham over cheese. Spread thinly with mustard. Place shoots in the middle and roll. Secure with toothpicks.
4. Place rolls in ovenproof dish. Add enough wine to cover bottom with 3/4 inch (2 cm) of liquid.
5. Bake until cheese melts, approximately 15 minutes.
6. The rolls can be served with or without Wine Sauce.

Wine sauce
Pour cooking liquid into a small saucepan. Bring to a boil. Thicken with beurre manié or with 1 teaspoon (5 mL) corn starch diluted in a little white wine or cold water.

Beurre manié: Combine equal amounts of soft butter and flour. Add to sauces and soups to thicken them.

Cattail Pollen Soufflé

Makes 4 servings (microwave)

This subtle dish is as golden, as light, and as delicious as a summer day.

Ingredients

1/2 cup (125 mL) butter
1 cup (250 mL) flour
salt
pepper
1/2 cup (125 mL) milk
1 cup (250 mL) cattail pollen
4 eggs, separated
1 cup (250 mL) strong Cheddar cheese, grated
1/4 cup (60 mL) mixed chopped herbs (tarragon, dill, parsley, chervil...)

Method

1. Preheat oven to 400°F (200°C).
2. In a saucepan, melt butter over low heat. Stir in flour, salt and pepper. Blend and cook for 2 to 3 minutes, then gradually whisk in milk. Stir until the sauce is thickened and smooth. Cool slightly.
3. Add cattail pollen, egg yolks, cheese and herbs.
4. Beat egg whites with a pinch of salt until stiff, then gently fold into mixture.
5. Pour mixture into greased soufflé dish and bake for 30 minutes. Avoid opening the oven door during cooking. Serve immediately.

Cattail pollen can be kept in the freezer (in a glass or plastic container) for up to one year. More recipes using cattail pollen are to be found in the Berries section.

Cream of Sorrel

Makes 4 servings

Ready in a few minutes, this light and tangy soup can be served hot or cold.

Ingredients
2 tbsp (30 mL) butter
1 cup (250 mL) tightly packed sheep sorrel
2 cups (500 mL) chicken stock
3 medium potatoes, peeled and diced
1 tbsp (15 mL) heavy cream or sour cream (optional)

Method
1. In a saucepan, melt butter. Add sorrel and stir 30 seconds.
2. Add chicken stock and potatoes. Bring to a boil, reduce heat and simmer until potatoes are cooked. Purée in blender.
3. Serve with a swirl of cream.

Sheep sorrel is dioecious. In other words, the male and female flowers bloom on separate plants.

Salmon and Sheep Sorrel Mousse
Makes 4 servings

Now, you can't make a more simple or more delicious dish than this one, which proves you don't need to move heaven and earth to eat like a god.

Ingredients

Puff pastry
1 cup (250 mL) water
1/4 cup (60 mL) butter
1 cup (250 mL) flour
4 eggs

1 can (7-1/2 oz/213 g) salmon
1 cup (250 mL) buttermilk
3 egg whites
salt

Sauce
1 cup (250 mL) heavy cream
1 cup (250 mL) sheep sorrel, chopped
salt
pepper

Method
1. Preheat oven to 375°F (190°C).
2. To prepare puff pastry, combine water and butter in a heavy saucepan and bring to a boil. Add flour all at once and stir rapidly with a wooden spoon until mixture forms a ball and leaves side of pan clean.
3. Remove from heat and add eggs, beating after each addition until glossy. Set aside.
4. Drain salmon. Discard skin and bones, then process in food processor until smooth. Add buttermilk and puff pastry.
5. Beat egg whites with a pinch of salt until stiff. Fold delicately into salmon mixture.
6. Pour into individual buttered baking dishes (ramekins). Stand dishes in a pan containing 1-1/8 inches (3 cm) of hot water and bake for 25 minutes or until a toothpick inserted in the middle comes out clean. Or bake in microwave oven 5 minutes at High.
7. To make the sauce, purée cream and sorrel in a food processor or a blender. Add salt and pepper and warm slowly over medium heat. Do not boil. Pour over the mousse. Serve with rice.

Puff pastry is easy to make and very versatile. To make puffs, drop dough by the spoonful onto a baking sheet, or use a pastry bag to make small round balls. Bake at 375°F (190°C) until golden and puffy, approximately 25 minutes. Prick each puff with a sharp knife to let heat escape, and let dry in open oven for 10 minutes. Garnish with sweet or salty preparations.

Potted Salmon

Makes 4 to 6 appetizer servings

This mixture is ideal for picnics. Spread it on herb scones or dig in with pita bread.

Ingredients

1 cup (250 mL) white wine
1 bay leaf
6 peppercorns
pinch nutmeg
salt
pepper
9 oz (250 g) salmon fillet
1/2 cup (125 mL) sour cream
2 tbsp (30 mL) minced mint
2 tbsp (30 mL) lemon juice

Method

1. In a small saucepan, preferably glass or ceramic, combine wine, bay leaf, peppercorns, nutmeg, salt and pepper. Simmer 5 minutes.
2. Add salmon and enough water to cover. Poach 8 to 10 minutes or until fish is no longer translucent.
3. Transfer to plate and cool. Strain cooking liquid and reduce over medium heat until 2 tablespoons (30 mL) remain.
4. Remove skin, bones and dark meat from the salmon. Flake fish into the bowl of a food processor. Add cooking liquid and process with short on/off pulses. Add sour cream, mint and lemon juice, and process intermittently to preserve the texture of the fish. Season to taste.
5. Transfer the mixture into a crock, smooth top with a spatula and chill several hours.
6. Remove from refrigerator 30 minutes before serving.

Lamb and Mint Rolls

Makes 10 rolls

Lamb and mint seem to be made for each other.

Ingredients

1 cup (250 mL) cooked lamb's quarters or spinach, finely chopped (see page 57)
1 onion, minced
olive oil
7 oz (200 g) minced lamb
1 egg
4 tbsp (60 mL) fresh mint, finely chopped
salt
pepper
10 sheets filo pastry

Method

1. Preheat oven to 375° F (190° C).
2. Cook onion in a little olive oil until soft. Add lamb and stir over medium heat for 2 to 3 minutes. The meat should stay pink.
3. In a large bowl, mix lamb's quarters or spinach with lamb, egg and mint. Season with salt and pepper.
4. Spread out one sheet of filo pastry (keep remaining pastry covered with a damp towel or plastic wrap to prevent drying). Brush with olive oil and cover with a second pastry sheet. Cut in two, lengthwise. Place 1 tablespoon (15 mL) of lamb filling at narrow end of strip. Tuck in sides and roll up. Seal ends with oil. Repeat with remaining filling.
5. Bake for 25 to 30 minutes or until golden. Serve with Yogurt Dressing (see page 79).

Wild Mushrooms

I cannot insist enough on the necessity of identifying wild mushrooms correctly. Rare are the really toxic ones, but you only need one.

I learned to identify mushrooms with the *Guide pratique des principaux champignons du Québec*, the bible of mushroom pickers in Quebec, and with the help of generous pickers. Generous, indeed, as mushroom sites are jealously guarded secrets! "You may ask for my car, you may even ask for my wife," says the old French picker (who never learned to be politically correct), "but don't ask me where I pick morels."

So if you find a generous soul, ready to show you some secret mushroom spots, treat this person well and count your blessings.

Another way to learn to identify fungi is to join a mycology club near you—they are growing like mushrooms. A visit to your local market can also be enlightening as certain species, mostly chanterelles and boletes, are now available fresh—for a king's ransom, I might add! Some, like oyster mushrooms, are commercially grown, though they do not have the flavor of the wild ones.

Collecting

Beginners are intimidated by the apparent complexity of the world of fungi. There are many shapes and colors to sort out. But don't get discouraged. It is actually quite easy to identify them.

Wild mushrooms are divided into categories according to their physical characteristics. The shape, color and texture of the cap, the features of the underside—whether it is covered with gills, spines or pores—the appearance of the stem and how it is attached to the cap are all keys to identification.

Most mushrooms grow in humus-rich earth in woods, although some prefer dry, open fields. Some mushrooms form symbiotic relationships with trees and will be found under one specific species. A knowledge of the growing season and the appropriate habitat will increase your chances of finding mushrooms.

While we associate mushroom picking with fall, foraging actually starts in May with morels. After a lull of a couple of months, chanterelles start to appear, usually in the middle of July, followed by boletes and others. Mushroom season continues until well into October, depending on the area.

When picking mushrooms, walk slowly and carry a sharp knife. Do not tear the mushroom from the ground; instead, cut the stem at the base. Try to remember where you find prize specimens as they often grow in the same spot year after year.

Pick young or mature mushrooms that are firm and untouched by animals. Remove surface dirt, pine needles, and other debris and place the mushrooms in a basket or a paper bag—never in a plastic bag—sorted by species, if possible. This saves cleaning time later, because some mushroom varieties are usually quite clean while others have more dirt on them.

Once home, clean the mushrooms thoroughly and refrigerate in a paper bag.

Cooking and Preserving

Some mushrooms are best eaten fresh; others develop their full flavor only when dried. For example, the fairy ring mushroom is quite insignificant when fresh but becomes a real delight once dry.

Fresh mushrooms should be prepared simply—lightly sautéed in butter and herbs —to bring out their delicate flavor. They can also serve as pancake or vol-au-vent (puff pastry) garnish. Dried mushrooms can withstand lengthy cooking and are ideal for stews and braised meat.

Chanterelles, hedgehog mushrooms and boletes freeze remarkably well, though the first two acquire a slight bitterness in the process, which is easily eliminated by blanching the frozen mushrooms in two changes of water before they are used.

Meadow mushroom

My Favorite Mushrooms

There are thousands of edible mushrooms but only a handful that are of real culinary interest. Some may be too soft or too small, or become tough or turn to mush when cooked. Others have no taste or are bitter, without being toxic. In short, you don't need to know many species, just the good ones.

Meadow mushroom
Agaricus campestris

This wild cousin of the commercial white mushroom is found almost exclusively in the open in rich pastures and city parks. It grows sometimes in circles, which are called fairy rings. I used to pick tons of meadow mushrooms on golf courses until I discovered how much pesticide, herbicide and other-cides are dumped on links to keep them green and weed free.

The bolete family
Boletaceae

Gourmets call them by their Italian name, porcini, or French name, cèpes. They are easily identifiable by their underside, which is covered with pores (tubes) instead of gills. Though there are many species of boletes, the king bolete (*Boletus edulis*) is the most sought after. Boletes grow in summer and fall, in moss-rich woodlands.

Chanterelle
Cantharellus spp.

The common chanterelle (*C. cibarius*) is definitely my favorite mushroom. Yellowish in color with hints of orange, its sweet, delicate fragrance is of roses and dried apricots. The genus includes the trumpet chanterelle (*C. tubaeformis*) and club-shaped chanterelle (*C. clavatus*). The horn of plenty (*Craterellus cornucopioides*) is a relative of the chanterelle genus. Most have a funnel-shaped cap, with gill-like ridges along the stem. Generally chanterelles grow in wet coniferous woods, but also may be found near deciduous trees.

The bolete family

Chanterelle

Golden clavaria
Ramaria aurea

A strange genus, *Ramaria*. Shaped like clubs, sponges, cauliflower or coral, these mushrooms have no cap and no stem but are branched. Some members may cause stomach upset. I pick the golden clavaria in coniferous and mixed woodlands. As this species is rather tasteless when fresh, I dry the branches and add them to stews and sauces.

Shaggy mane
Coprinus comatus

Now, here is an easily identifiable and common mushroom. You have certainly seen its elegant clusters on lawns and along country roads. White as snow when it emerges, the shaggy mane grows quickly up to 8 inches (20 cm) in height. And just as quickly it turns gray, then black, and melts into an inky substance. Picked young and cooked immediately, the shaggy mane has a delicate flavor. Sauté shaggy manes in butter and herbs or add them to tomato sauce.

Hedgehog mushroom
Hydnum repandum

Fleshy and subtle in taste, the hedgehog mushroom is another favorite of mine. Sometimes misshapen when growing in clusters, it can be identified by the spines covering the underside of the cap. This species loves the mossy floor of coniferous woodlands. The hedgehog mushroom can be frozen, but, because it then acquires a bitter taste, it should be blanched before using.

Fairy ring mushroom
Marasmus oreades

The name "fairy ring" refers to this species' growing pattern, a characteristic circle found on lawns and grassy areas. Better tasting when dried, the fairy ring mushroom can be dried, reduced to a powder and used as a condiment.

Beware! The toxic sweat-producing clitocybe (*Clitocybe dealbata*) grows in the same habitat but can be easily identified by its closely spaced gills running some way down the stem. Fairy ring mushrooms have fairly well-spaced gills appearing almost free from the stem.

Golden clavaria

Shaggy mane

Hedgehog mushroom

Fairy ring mushroom

Oyster mushroom

The russula family

The puffball family

Morel

Oyster mushroom
Pleurotus ostreatus

Don't look on the ground for this mushroom. It grows in tiers or rows on deciduous trees and occasionally on conifers. The caps vary in color from cream to dark gray, and the gills are soft and cream colored. Available commercially, oyster mushrooms can also be grown at home. The medium on which they grow is a log that must be kept moist. With proper care, oyster mushrooms are supposed to grow again and again if harvested regularly. I have tried to grow them, and I confess I didn't have much luck. I forgot to water the log, or I waited too long to harvest them.

The russula family
Russulaceae

Russulas grow with deciduous and coniferous trees, on dry as well as wet land. I call these "cartoon mushrooms" as they come in bright red, orange, yellow, blue, mauve, pink, green, gray and all shades in between. The green, blue and yellow russulas are the most sought after. Not all russulas are edible. The emetic russula (*Russula emetica*), which has a red cap, is toxic; others (mostly red) are bitter or acrid.

Young russulas keep three or four days in the fridge in a paper bag.

The puffball family
Lycoperdaceae

Puffballs grow mostly in grassy areas such as lawns, open parks, golf courses and pastures. Some, like the stump puffball, can be found in deciduous woods. The giant puffball (*Calvatia gigantea*) can grow up to 28 inches (70 cm) across. The warted puffball (*Lycoperdon perlatum*) is rarely more than 2 inches (5 cm) in width. Both are delicious when fresh. Sauté slices of the giant puffball in butter and herbs; slice the warted puffball and add it raw to salads.

Morel
Morchella esculenta

I must admit I find morels rather tasteless compared with boletes or chanterelles—perhaps morels wouldn't be so sought after if they were not so rare. Morels grow in spring, often in abandoned apple orchards or under poplars, and are best when dried.

The morel should not be confused with *Gyromitra esculenta*, or false morel, which is sometimes considered toxic. False morel actually is edible as long as it is blanched before cooking and the cooking water thrown away.

Blini with Trumpet Chanterelles

Makes 4 servings

Blini are small buckwheat pancakes. This Russian delicacy is traditionally served with caviar, here replaced by trumpet chanterelles.

Ingredients

Pancake batter
1/2 cup (125 mL) flour
1/4 cup (60 mL) buckwheat flour
1 tsp (5 mL) baking powder
1/2 tsp (2 mL) salt
1 cup (250 mL) milk
2 eggs
cooking oil

Topping
2 tbsp (30 mL) butter
4 cups (1 L) trumpet chanterelles
salt
pepper
1/2 cup (125 mL) heavy cream

Method

1. Combine flours, baking powder and salt. In a separate bowl, beat together milk and eggs. Stir into flour mixture and beat until batter is smooth. Refrigerate for 2 hours. After refrigerating, the batter should lightly coat a spoon; dilute with cold water if too thick.
2. In a heavy skillet or nonstick pan, make small, thin pancakes. Keep warm.
3. Meanwhile, melt butter in heavy saucepan. Add chanterelles, cover and simmer 3 minutes. Season with salt and pepper. Just before serving, add cream to mushrooms. Bring to a boil then remove from heat.
4. Arrange blini on serving plates. Top with mushrooms.

Trumpet chanterelles grow in clusters, sometimes quite dense, in mossy coniferous woodlands. These mushrooms freeze well, keeping their shape and flavor.

Beef Stroganoff

Makes 4 servings

In Eastern European countries, mushroom picking is a favorite pastime.

Ingredients
10 oz (300 g) beef fillet or sandwich steak
3 tbsp (45 mL) butter
1 onion
2 cups (500 mL) mushrooms (boletes, meadow mushrooms, russulas, chanterelles)
1 tbsp (15 mL) oil
cognac
1 cup (250 mL) heavy cream
salt
pepper
parsley, chopped

Method
1. Cut beef into strips. Mince onion and slice mushrooms.
2. Melt 1 tablespoon (15 mL) of the butter in a heavy skillet and sauté onion until soft. Add mushrooms, cover and simmer a couple of minutes until mushrooms are half cooked. Reserve.
3. Wipe pan clean and heat remaining butter with oil. Sauté meat 1 minute over high heat, stirring continuously. Pour in a dash of cognac and flambé. Add onion mixture and cream and mix well. Bring to a boil and cook 1 minute.
4. Season with salt and pepper to taste. Sprinkle with fresh chopped parsley and serve with steamed new potatoes or fresh noodles.

Stuffed Cèpes (Porcini)

Makes 4 servings

Here is a winning combination: Stuffed Cèpes (porcini mushrooms), Yarrow-flavored Goat Cheese and Oven-dried Tomatoes.

Ingredients

12 medium size boletes*
1/2 cup (125 mL) garlic-flavored croutons, crumbled
4 tbsp (60 mL) soft butter
2 tbsp (30 mL) chopped parsley
1 green onion, minced
bread crumbs
oil or melted butter

Method

1. Clean mushrooms. Cut stems and chop half finely (freeze remaining stems to use in soups or stuffings). Combine with croutons, butter, parsley and green onion.
2. Stuff caps with mushroom mixture. Sprinkle with bread crumbs. Drizzle with oil or melted butter. Broil a few minutes until sizzling. Serve hot.

*Russulas, meadow mushrooms or commercially grown mushrooms can be substituted.

Yarrow-flavored Goat Cheese: Place small, fresh goat cheese in a glass jar with a handful of yarrow leaves. Cover with olive oil. Marinate a couple of days.

Oven-dried Tomatoes: Cut round tomatoes in quarters, Italian tomatoes in half. Arrange on a baking sheet and dry in oven at lowest temperature (180°F/80°C), 18 to 24 hours, depending on water content. Keep in glass jars, tightly sealed. To serve, soak in warm water until soft. Drain, pressing with spoon to remove all liquid. Marinate in olive oil, herbs, crushed garlic, salt and pepper.

Cèpe Consommé

Makes 4 servings

A delight for the eye as well as the palate, this stunning consommé is the perfect introduction to a gourmet dinner.

Ingredients

1 cup (250 mL) dried boletes
6 cups (1.5 L) beef stock
1 bouquet garni (thyme, bay leaf, marjoram, rosemary)
4 tbsp (60 mL) Madeira
salt
pepper

Method

1. Soak mushrooms in warm water for 1 hour.
2. Bring stock to a boil with bouquet garni and cook 5 minutes.
3. Add mushrooms and soaking liquid to stock. Simmer 15 minutes. Remove mushrooms and arrange in serving bowls. Filter consommé through cheesecloth. Add Madeira, salt and pepper.
4. Pour consommé over mushrooms and serve.

Note: You may want to clarify the consommé for a better appearance. Prepare consommé in advance and cool. Remove mushrooms. Beat 1 egg white until frothy and add to consommé. Heat slowly and simmer 5 minutes, whisking frequently. The egg white will pick up particles floating in the liquid. Remove from heat and let settle 5 minutes before straining consommé through cheesecloth.

Bouquet garni: This is the French term for assorted aromatic herbs tied in a bunch and added to soups and stews for flavor. Generally, bouquet garni is composed of parsley, bay leaf, thyme, and rosemary, but can also include cloves, savory, lovage, sage or the white part of leeks. If using dried herbs, place in a piece of cheesecloth and tie securely. Remove bouquet garni before the dish is served.

Veal Rolls with Mushroom Sauce

Makes 4 servings

The earthy flavor of wild mushrooms works well with veal, and the cheese brings creaminess to these quick and easy meat rolls.

Ingredients
1 cup (250 mL) dried golden clavaria
2 tbsp (30 mL) soft butter
salt
pepper
4 veal cutlets
4 slices Gruyère or mozzarella cheese
2 tbsp (30 mL) butter
2 tbsp (30 mL) oil
1/4 cup (60 mL) white wine
1 cup (250 mL) fresh boletes, chanterelles or meadow mushrooms, minced

Method
1. Soak clavaria in warm water for 1 hour.
2. Drain and press to extract all liquid. Chop finely and add to soft butter. Season with salt and pepper.
3. Pound veal until thin or ask your butcher to do it. Place a slice of cheese over each cutlet. Spread with one-quarter of the stuffing, leaving edges free. Roll up tightly and tie with kitchen string or secure with toothpicks.
4. Heat butter and oil in heavy skillet. Cook rolls, turning occasionally until golden. Add wine and a little water. Cover and simmer 10 minutes. Add fresh mushrooms and cook 5 more minutes.
5. Remove rolls and keep warm. Add 1 teaspoon (5 mL) beurre manié (see page 71) to sauce and heat slowly, stirring until thickened. Pour over rolls and serve.

Russulas, Lyonnaise Style

Makes 2 servings

This hearty fall dish makes a quick and easy vegetarian meal or can be served with grilled sausages. Lyonnaise style refers to preparations with onions sautéed in butter and deglazed with vinegar.

Ingredients
3 tbsp (45 mL) butter
2 tbsp (30 mL) oil
1 onion, thickly sliced
2 cups (500 mL) new potatoes, cooked and cubed
salt, pepper
2 cups (500 mL) russulas, in chunks
2 tbsp (30 mL) balsamic vinegar (optional)
parsley, thyme, rosemary, or oregano, chopped

Method
1. Heat butter and oil in a heavy skillet and sauté onion until soft. Add potatoes, salt and pepper to taste and sauté over medium heat for 5 minutes.
2. Add russulas, cover and cook 3 minutes.
3. Before serving, drizzle with balsamic vinegar, if using, and herbs.

Tomato Sauce with Shaggy Manes

Makes 4 servings

Blessed is the gardener who sees shaggy manes grow on the lawn.

Ingredients
1 onion, minced
1/4 cup (60 mL) olive oil
4 cups (1 L) shaggy manes, thickly sliced
4 large ripe tomatoes, peeled and chopped
salt, pepper
4 basil leaves, chopped

Method
1. Sauté onion in oil until soft. Add mushrooms. Cook over high heat for 2 minutes.
2. Add tomatoes, season with salt and pepper and cook over medium heat until thick.
3. Sprinkle with basil and serve over fettuccini.

Minute Pizza: Spread sauce over pita bread. Sprinkle with grated cheese and fresh herbs. Drizzle with olive oil. Broil until cheese is melted.

Oriental Stir-fry

Makes 4 servings

Chinese cooks use many different kinds of dried mushrooms. You will find them in Asian markets.

Ingredients

Marinade
1/4 cup (60 mL) soy sauce
1/4 cup (60 mL) water
2 tbsp (30 mL) sesame oil
1 tbsp (15 mL) fresh ginger juice (see page 42)

1 chicken breast, cubed
2 tbsp (30 mL) oil
1 onion, thickly sliced
2 carrots, sliced diagonally
1/2 cup (125 mL) dried Chinese mushrooms or dried boletes
1 cup (250 mL) broccoli flowerettes or zucchini slices
1 cup (250 mL) miniature corn cobs
1/2 cup (125 mL) water chestnuts, sliced
1/4 cup (60 mL) cashew nuts
1 package (16 oz/454 g) Chinese egg noodles

Method

1. Combine all marinade ingredients. Pour over chicken cubes and refrigerate 30 minutes.
2. In a large skillet or wok, heat oil. Drain chicken cubes and stir-fry until just firm. Set aside.
3. Add more oil to the pan if necessary and stir-fry onion for 1 minute. Add carrots, mushrooms, broccoli, corn cobs, water chestnuts and cashews. Cover and cook 5 minutes over medium heat.
4. Meanwhile, cook noodles.
5. Add chicken and marinade to vegetable mixture and stir-fry 1 minute.
6. Serve on a bed of egg noodles.

Chinese Soup with Fairy Ring Mushrooms

Makes 2 servings

Asian soups are a meal in a bowl and, in my humble opinion, the best fast food ever invented.

Ingredients

Marinade
2 tbsp (30 mL) soy sauce
2 tbsp (30 mL) sesame oil
1 tbsp (15 mL) fresh ginger juice (see page 42)

1/2 chicken breast, cubed
1/2 cup (125 mL) dried fairy ring mushrooms
2 tbsp (30 mL) oil
2 cups (500 mL) chicken stock
1/2 cup (125 mL) lamb's quarters or spinach, chopped
1/3 cup (75 mL) fresh or frozen green peas
1 cup (250 mL) cooked Chinese rice noodles or vermicelli

Method

1. Mix marinade and marinate chicken. Soak mushrooms in warm water while preparing other ingredients.
2. Stir-fry chicken cubes in oil 1 minute. Reserve.
3. Bring chicken stock to a boil. Add lamb's quarters or spinach, peas, noodles and mushrooms, drained of their water. Bring back to a boil and add chicken. Cook 1 minute.
4. Serve soup in large bowls, with a dash of sesame oil and soy sauce.

Japanese Soup

Makes 2 servings

Here is another example of a meal in a bowl.

Ingredients
3-1/2 oz (100 g) udon noodles* or fettuccini
2 eggs
2 cups (500 mL) chicken stock
1/2 cup (125 mL) broccoli flowerettes
1/2 cup (125 mL) wild mushrooms (boletes, chanterelles, meadow mushrooms...)
sesame oil
soy sauce
hiziki (optional)

Method
1. Cook noodles. Rinse and set aside.
2. Poach eggs in stock. Add noodles, broccoli and mushrooms. Cook a couple of minutes.
3. Serve with a dash of sesame oil and soy sauce, and sprinkle with rehydrated hiziki (see below).

*Udon noodles are thick Japanese noodles made with flour and used in soups. Spaghetti makes an acceptable equivalent if udon noodles are unavailable.

Hiziki is a black seaweed similar in form to angel hair noodles. Sold dried, it must be soaked in water before use.

Seaweed is an excellent source of vitamins and minerals. Several species are edible. Dulse, Irish moss, kelp, laver and sea lettuce can be gathered and eaten fresh or dried.

Seaweed is available in Asian markets and health food stores.

Tomatoes Stuffed with Russulas

Makes 2 to 4 servings

Tomatoes ripen when russulas appear. Combine them in this sunny and mouthwatering dish.

Ingredients
1 onion, minced
olive oil
1 cup (250 mL) russulas, chopped
1 cup (250 mL) cooked rice
1/2 cup (125 mL) chopped parsley
2 eggs
salt
pepper
4 ripe tomatoes
bread crumbs

Method
1. Preheat oven to 375°F (190°C).
2. Cook onion in oil until soft. Add russulas, cover and simmer 2 minutes.
3. In a bowl, combine mushroom mixture, rice, parsley and eggs. Season with salt and pepper.
4. Cut the top off the tomatoes and scoop out the inside. Stuff with mushroom mixture. Sprinkle top with bread crumbs and drizzle with oil.
5. Place tomatoes in greased ovenproof dish. Bake for 30 minutes.
6. Serve with a green salad.

Use the same mixture to stuff other vegetables such as zucchini, onions or eggplants. Partially cook these vegetables before stuffing them. Add their pulp to the mushroom mixture.

Tortellini with Artichoke Hearts and Shaggy Manes

Makes 4 to 6 servings

Northern Italy is famous for its wild mushrooms. In summer and fall, dozens of pickers can be seen foraging in fields and forests.

Ingredients

1 package (7 oz/200 g) cheese-filled tortellini
1 onion, minced
2 tbsp (30 mL) olive oil
2 cups (500 mL) shaggy manes or other wild mushrooms, sliced
1 can (14 oz/398 mL) artichoke hearts, drained and sliced
2 tomatoes, chopped
salt
pepper
fresh basil or oregano

Method

1. Cook tortellini following package instructions. Drain.
2. Cook onion in oil until soft. Add mushrooms, artichoke hearts and tomatoes. Season with salt and pepper. Cover and cook 5 minutes.
3. Add tortellini and heat thoroughly. Sprinkle with herbs before serving.

The Ink-cap (Coprinus atramentarus), another member of the Coprinus family, is a fleshy mushroom that often grows in large clusters. This Coprinus also is edible, BUT alcohol should not be consumed either with a meal containing it or during the following 24 hours, as skin rash, nausea and palpitations may occur.

Leg of Lamb with Hedgehog Mushrooms
Makes 2 servings

Though I usually shy away from heavy cream, I couldn't make this creamy sauce any other way.

Ingredients
1 tbsp (15 mL) butter
1 tbsp (15 mL) oil
2 slices of leg of lamb
2 cups (500 mL) hedgehog mushrooms in chunks
1/2 cup (125 mL) heavy cream
salt
pepper

Method
1. In a large frying pan, heat butter and oil. Brown lamb 2 minutes on each side. Remove and keep warm.
2. Add mushrooms to pan, cover and cook 2 minutes at medium heat.
3. Pour in cream and stir to mix with the lamb juice. Season with salt and pepper. Add meat to pan, cover and cook until done.
4. Serve with rice or fresh noodles.

Hedgehog mushrooms stay firm for several days if kept in a brown paper bag and refrigerated. They can also be frozen but should be blanched in 2 changes of water before cooking.

Microwave blanching: Put frozen mushrooms in bowl, cover with water and microwave 3 minutes at High. Drain water and repeat.

Trout with Meadow Mushrooms
Makes 4 servings

The fish can be stuffed and refrigerated until cooking time.

Ingredients
1 onion, finely chopped
2 tbsp (30 mL) butter
1 cup (250 mL) meadow mushrooms or white mushrooms, chopped
1/4 cup (60 mL) bread crumbs
2 tbsp (30 mL) parsley, minced
salt
pepper
4 small trout, cleaned and boned

Method
1. Cook onion in 1 tablespoon (15 mL) of the butter until soft. Add mushrooms and cook 1 minute. Add bread crumbs and parsley. Season with salt and pepper.
2. Fill each trout with mushroom mixture.
3. Melt remaining butter in large pan. Cook trout 2 minutes on each side. Cover and cook over low heat until done, approximately 10 minutes.

Serve with Lamb's Quarters Flan (see page 60).

Chanterelles Ramekins

Serve this ultra-quick and easy dish for breakfast or a light supper.

Ingredients

Per ramekin (microwave)
1 tbsp (15 mL) butter
3 tbsp (45 mL) chanterelles, sliced
1 egg
3 tbsp (45 mL) heavy cream or sour cream
minced parsley
salt
pepper

Method

1. Place butter and chanterelles in ramekin. Beat egg with cream and pour over mushrooms. Season with parsley, salt and pepper.
2. Cook in microwave 2 minutes on High.
3. Serve with French bread.

Replace chanterelles with bacon bits, artichoke hearts or cheese. Use tomato sauce or salsa instead of cream.

Berries and Other Fruits

There is something about picking berries that evokes summer—long, hot days, smiles smeared with juice, scrumptious desserts and happy childhood memories.

There is no simpler pleasure than walking, basket in hand, through sweet-smelling fields in search of blackberries. And nothing compares to the taste of raspberries freshly picked off the cane.

Through the summer and until late in the fall, all kinds of small fruits and berries appear in succession to feed birds, small mammals and big ones, such as bears...and us too!

There are over 200 species of small fruits growing wild in Canada and the northern United States. Most are rich in vitamin C, but also contain calcium, iron, vitamin A, thiamin, riboflavin and niacin.

Some berries, such as bearberry and cranberry, remain on the plants throughout the winter, making them an important source of emergency food.

Native people made extensive use of small fruits and berries, eating them raw or cooked or drying them for use in winter. Pemmican is made with dried fruits, dried meat or fish and fat.

Berries

Blackberry
Rubus spp.

The Rubus genus is large and includes blackberries, raspberries, dewberries and many others. They are found in sunny thickets and open woods, in parts of Canada and the northern United States. Blackberries ripen in August.

Blueberry
Vaccinium myrtilloides and *V. angustifolium*

Early low blueberry (*V. angustifolium*) is a plant with large fruit. Sourtop blueberry (*V. myrtilloides*) is a plant with small fruit. Both are rich in vitamin A and C. During World War II, blueberry extract was given to RAF pilots to improve their night vision. Blueberry syrup is said to relieve diarrhea.

Blueberries grow in a wide range of habitats, from coastal regions to mountain summits, in woods, peat bogs and alpine slopes. Most prefer a moist soil and a sunny location. They are particularly abundant in areas cleared by fire.

Bunchberry
Cornus canadensis

This charming little plant covers mountain slopes and river banks, mossy woods and rocky shores, wherever there are conifers. The white starlike flowers of early summer become clusters of red berries, and although not very flavorful, they're a nice snack when you're on the trail. Easy and quick to pick, bunchberries make colorful pies.

Cranberry
Vaccinium spp.

Cranberry is the name given to several types of wild berries, including the bog cranberry (*V. oxycoccus*), ancestor of the cultivated cranberry and the lingonberry (*V. vitis-idaea*), also called mountain cranberry.

Members of the heather family, cranberries are low, creeping evergreen bushes that grow in bogs and peaty soil. The berries are red to purplish when ripe. They become juicier and softer after the first frost. Use them fresh as you would commercial cranberries, or substitute dry cranberries in recipes requiring raisins.

Blackberry

Bunchberry

Gooseberry

There are about a dozen species of wild gooseberry growing in Canada and the northern United States. This cousin of the currant likes the partial shade of open woods and the edge of forests. Most species have thorny branches and fuzzy fruits. Luckily, the most wide-spread is the smooth gooseberry (*Ribes hirtellum*), a handsome bush that can grow up to six feet if transplanted to well-drained soil in the garden. In spring, small, yellow, bell-shaped flowers appear in clusters. The berries, which are bluish black with tough, pointed tails, ripen in August. All gooseberries make wonderful jams, jellies and preserves, and also sauces for meat and venison.

Common elderberry
Sambuccus canadensis

This tall, elegant shrub is found in damp, rich soil in eastern and central North America. After a spectacular display of creamy white flowers in June, there follows a crop of tiny, black fruits in heavy clusters that weigh down the branches. Elderberries are easy picking.

Seedy and tart, the fruits are mildly unpleasant when eaten raw but make an excellent jelly when mixed with the juice of other fruits rich in pectin (apples, half-ripe grapes, crab-apples).

Elderberry can be grown from seed or propagated by layering.

Highbush cranberry
Viburnum trilobum

This tall shrub, a relative of the ornamental snowball bush of our gardens, is not to be con-fused with cranberries of the genus *Vaccinum*. Called "pimbina" by Aboriginal people, it is found in cool woods and thickets and along shores in Canada and the northern United States. Bright red fruits are borne in the fall. Hard and very sour, they become softer and more palatable when touched by frost. The berries are rich in vitamin C, and are excellent when cooked with sugar and made into sauce for poultry and game, or into jelly. Remove seeds for a more pleasant texture.

Gooseberry

Common elderberry

Raspberry

Strawberry

Raspberry
Rubus spp.

Very similar to its cultivated counterpart, if somewhat smaller, the wild raspberry grows everywhere on the continent, except on the tundra and in the Pacific rainforest, in open woods and fields.

There are red raspberries and black raspberries (also called thimbleberries), which should not be confused with blackberries. Black raspberries have more seeds than the red variety and are preferable for making jellies.

Raspberry leaves make a diuretic and tonic tea. Pick the leaves in spring when they are young and tender, or in late fall when they have turned red. A decoction made from raspberry leaves can be used as skin lotion and as a gargle for mouth infections.

Strawberry
Fragaria virginiana

In my area, wild strawberries are tiny and lack flavor, and, in my humble opinion, are not worth picking. But in other areas, when they are fleshy and fully ripe, wild strawberries are a real treat. They are found almost everywhere in fields and open places. Wild strawberries are easy to transplant to the garden where they make a pretty ground cover.

Other Fruits

Apple

Not really wild but remnants of old orchards, wild apples come in many colors and tastes. More tart than the domestic variety, and often scabbed and ridden with worms, wild apples are nevertheless an excellent source of pectin for use in jams or jellies. They also make succulent butters.

Serviceberry
Amelanchier spp.

There are about 15 species of *Amelanchier*, all of them eastern in distribution except *A. alnifolia*, the saskatoon berry, which is a western species. Serviceberry, Juneberry and shadbush all refer to the same plant, which has small, round fruits that are purple to black and have a pearlike taste. Saskatoon berries—the name is a Cree word—are most prevalent on the Prairies where they can reach the size of grapes. The shrub is quite decorative, especially when in bloom in spring, and is available from nurseries. The berries are eaten raw or cooked.

Riverbank grape
Vitis riparia

This prolific vine—prolific in stems and leaves at least—grows throughout eastern and central North America along country roads, in thickets and at the edges of woods. Wild grapes are the size of blueberries, and the bunches are small, but plentiful in good years. They ripen in late fall and should be picked when the leaves have dried up. You'll have competition from migrating birds, which feast on them. Young tender leaves can be cooked—steam for 10 minutes—and eaten like greens, or stuffed in the Greek-style with vinegared rice.

In A.D. 992, Leif Ericsson, son of Eric the Red, and 35 Viking companions left the shores of Greenland and sailed west in search of a new land. When they arrived in North America— five centuries before Christopher Columbus—they discovered a rich land, Newfoundland, that they called Vinland. One may speculate that it was because of the abundance of wild grape.

Apple

Riverbank grape

Raspberry Cake

Makes 8 to 10 servings

This spectacular cake is so delicious, your family will ask for it again and again, and it is so easy to make, you won't be able to refuse.

Ingredients

1 cup (250 mL) oil
1 cup (250 mL) sugar
4 eggs
2 tsp (10 mL) vanilla
2 cups (500 mL) flour
1 cup (250 mL) cattail pollen
1-1/2 tsp (7 mL) baking powder
pinch salt
2 cups (500 mL) heavy cream
3 cups (750 mL) wild raspberries

Method

1. Preheat oven to 350°F (180°C).
2. Line three 9-inch (1 L) round baking pans with wax paper. Grease.
3. Beat oil and sugar together until creamy. Add eggs one at a time while beating, then vanilla.
4. Mix dry ingredients and combine with egg mixture. Beat until thoroughly mixed. Divide batter equally between pans.
5. Bake for 25 to 30 minutes until a toothpick comes out clean. Cool in pans for 5 minutes, remove from pan, remove wax paper and cool on wire.
6. Whip cream until soft peaks are formed. Add sugar to taste. Spread one-third of cream on cake. Cover with a layer of raspberries and repeat. Top with remaining cream and raspberries.

Muffins with Cattail Pollen

Makes about 10 muffins

Serve these golden muffins with Apple and Mint Jelly (see page 168).

Ingredients
1/4 cup (60 mL) butter
1/2 cup (125 mL) brown sugar
1/4 cup (60 mL) honey
2 eggs
1 tsp (5 mL) vanilla
1-1/2 cups (375 mL) flour
1 cup (250 mL) cattail pollen
1-1/2 tsp (7 mL) baking powder
1/2 tsp (2 mL) baking soda
pinch salt
1 cup (250 mL) milk

Garnishes (optional)
1 cup (250 mL) fresh elderberry flowers or
1/2 cup (125 mL) bunchberries or
1/2 cup (125 mL) raisins or dates

Method
1. Preheat oven to 375°F (190°C).
2. Beat butter and sugar together until creamy and light in color. Add honey, eggs and vanilla. Beat until well blended.
3. Sift together dry ingredients and add to butter mixture, alternating with milk until all is moistened and combined.
4. Fill muffin tins about two-thirds full. Bake for 25 minutes or until muffins are well risen and golden.

Omelette Soufflé with Wild Berries

Makes 2 servings

This elegant dessert is the perfect ending to a romantic dinner.

Ingredients
2 eggs, separated
1 tbsp (15 mL) sugar
1 tbsp (15 mL) Raspberry Liqueur (see page 150)
1 tbsp (15 mL) butter
1 cup (250 mL) wild berries (blueberries, raspberries, blackberries, gooseberries...)
icing sugar

Method
1. Preheat oven to 400°F (200°C).
2. Beat egg whites until stiff. Combine yolks, sugar and liqueur and beat well. With a spatula, fold in egg whites.
3. Melt butter in ovenproof skillet. Pour in batter and smooth top with spatula. Bake until fluffy and golden on the underside, approximately 2 minutes. Brown top under broiler for a few seconds.
4. Arrange berries in the middle of the omelette and fold delicately. Slide onto serving dish, sprinkle with icing sugar and drizzle with Raspberry Liqueur, if desired. Serve immediately.

Blueberry Pudding with Port Sauce

Makes 4 to 6 servings (microwave)

This heart-warming dessert is perfect for cold winter evenings.

2 cups (500 mL) blueberries or other berries
1-1/3 cups (325 mL) flour
1 tsp (5 mL) baking powder
1/2 cup (125 mL) honey
1/2 cup (125 mL) boiling water
1 tsp (5 mL) baking soda
heavy cream

1. Mix berries, flour and baking powder.
2. Combine honey, water and baking soda (it will fizzle) and add to dry ingredients. Mix well.
3. Pour mixture into 6-cup (1.5 L) buttered mold.
4. Cover with plastic film and microwave 10 minutes on High. Or cover with aluminum foil, secure with kitchen string and steam in a large saucepan partly full of water for 1-1/2 hours.
5. Unmold and serve with lightly whipped cream and Port Sauce.

Port Sauce
Slowly melt 1 cup (250 mL) Port and Wild Grape Jelly (see page 166). Pour over pudding.

Bunchberry Pie
Makes 4 to 6 servings

Bunchberries can be replaced by serviceberries or any other firm fruit.

Ingredients
Filling
1 cup (250 mL) raisins
1/2 cup (125 mL) sherry
2 cups (500 mL) bunchberries
1 tbsp (15 mL) flour
1/2 cup (125 mL) brown sugar
cinnamon
nutmeg
2 tbsp (30 mL) butter

Pie crust
2 cups (500 mL) flour
1 tsp (5 mL) salt
1/3 cup (80 mL) butter
1/3 cup (80 mL) shortening
cold water

Method
1. Preheat oven to 375°F (190°C).
2. Soak raisins in sherry.
3. In the meantime, clean and wash bunchberries.
4. Drain raisins* and add to bunchberries. Mix flour, sugar, cinnamon and nutmeg and add fruits.
5. Sift together flour and salt. Cut in butter and shortening, either by hand using two knives, or with a food processor, until the dough is the consistency of crumbs. Add cold water, a spoonful at a time, until dough holds together but is not sticky. Chill 1 hour.
6. Roll out dough and line a pie dish. Add filling. Dot with butter. Use remaining dough to make lattice top. Brush pastry with beaten egg or milk.
7. Bake for 25 minutes or until golden.

*Serve soaking liquid as an aperitif, over ice or mixed with orange juice.

Hazelnut-berry Tartlets
Makes 8 tartlets

These tarts are perfect for a picnic. Bring along the cooked tart shells and garnish with freshly picked berries.

Ingredients

Pastry dough
1/2 cup (125 mL) hazelnuts
1 cup (250 mL) flour
2 tbsp (30 mL) sugar
1/3 cup (80 mL) butter
2 to 4 tbsp (30 to 60 mL) milk

Filling
1 cup (250 mL) ricotta cheese
1 tbsp (15 mL) sugar
wild berries (blueberries, raspberries, blackberries)
grated peel of 1 orange

Method

1. Spread hazelnuts on a baking sheet or pan and bake at 350°F (180°C) for 10 minutes. Transfer to a tea towel and rub off the skins. In food processor or blender, pulse to chop finely.
2. Mix flour, hazelnuts and sugar. Cut in butter until the consistency of cornmeal. Add milk until dough holds together but is not wet. Chill 30 minutes to 1 hour.
3. Preheat oven to 400°F (200°C).
4. Roll out dough and line tartlet molds. Cover with aluminum foil.
5. Bake for 10 minutes. Remove aluminum foil and bake 5 minutes.
6. Combine ricotta, sugar and orange peel. Fill tartlets and garnish with berries. Can be served with a coulis.

Coulis

Cook 1 cup (250 mL) berries in a little water with 2 tablespoons (30 mL) of sugar for 5 minutes. Strain to remove seeds.

Cranberry Scones

Makes about 10 scones

Scones are Scottish in origin and traditionally served warm and buttered at high tea.

Ingredients

2 cups (500 mL) flour
1 tbsp (15 mL) sugar
1 tbsp (15 mL) baking powder
pinch salt
1/4 cup (60 mL) butter
1/2 cup (125 mL) wild cranberries (or commercial cranberries, cut in quarters)
1 egg
1/2 cup (125 mL) buttermilk or heavy cream

Method

1. Preheat oven to 400°F (200°C).
2. Combine flour, sugar, baking powder and salt. Work in butter until the consistency of crumbs. Add cranberries and toss.
3. Beat egg in buttermilk, add to dry mixture and mix to make a soft dough.
4. Turn dough out onto a slightly floured surface. Flatten to a thickness of 1 inch (2.5 cm). Cut scones with a cookie cutter. Brush with egg and sprinkle with sugar.
5. Bake for 15 minutes or until golden.

Cold Drinks and Liqueurs

Cool drinks for hot summer days, warm toddies for cold winter evenings—the range of preparations you can make with wild berries and herbs is wide and varied. Here are some suggestions that will delight both family and friends.

Florida Mint

Makes 4 servings

Here is my version of a Mint Julep, the southern cocktail traditionally served in silver goblets at the Kentucky Derby.

Ingredients

4 tbsp (60 mL) frozen orange juice concentrate
1/2 cup (125 mL) Jack Daniels or Bourbon
1/2 cup (125 mL) strawberries, fresh or frozen
1/4 cup (60 mL) chopped mint
1 cup (250 mL) water

Method

1. Mix all ingredients at high speed in a blender or a food processor, until frothy.
2. Strain and serve over crushed ice.

Kir à la Québécoise

In the 1960s, Chanoine Kir was mayor of Dijon, France, and would only serve one type of drink during official receptions. A combination of crème de cassis, a black currant flavored liqueur, and white Burgundy, this drink thus became known as Kir. Now if Chanoine Kir had lived in Quebec, he might have used Raspberry Liqueur (see page 150) and sparkling apple cider.

1. Pour a dash of Raspberry Liqueur into champagne glasses.
2. Fill with cider and serve chilled.

Lemonade from the Wild

Makes 4 cups (1 L)

Refreshing and slightly tangy, this lemonade is also a tonic, an ideal pick-me-up on hot summer days.

Ingredients

*1 cup (250 mL) boiling water
handful of young yarrow leaves
1 cup (250 mL) sheep sorrel
1/2 cup (125 mL) mint leaves
juice of 3 lemons
3 cups (750 mL) cold water
sugar*

Method

1. Pour boiling water over yarrow leaves. Steep 15 minutes. Strain and cool.
2. Put sorrel, mint, lemon juice and yarrow tea in blender or food processor. Process at high speed.
3. Strain. Add cold water and sugar to taste. Serve over crushed ice.

Raspberry Liqueur

Makes 2 cups (500 mL)

This ruby-red liqueur is as fragrant as a fresh raspberry.

Ingredients

2 cups (500 mL) wild raspberries
1-1/2 cups (375 mL) vodka
1 cup (250 mL) sugar

Method

1. In a glass jar, arrange layers of raspberries and sugar. Pour vodka over. Seal and place in the sun for 4 weeks. Strain.
2. If too sweet, dilute with brandy or vodka.
3. Keep in a cool, dark place. Drink within 3 months.

Mint-Raspberry Punch

Makes 2 servings

The cooling flavor of mint adds zing to this summer drink.

Ingredients

4 tbsp (60 mL) frozen orange juice concentrate
1 cup (250 mL) wild raspberries
1/2 cup (125 mL) mint leaves, minced
1 cup (250 mL) water
vodka or brandy (optional)

Method

1. In a blender or food processor, process all ingredients until frothy. Strain, pressing to get all the juices.
2. Add vodka or brandy, if desired. Serve chilled.

Mulled Delight
Makes 4 servings

Canned or frozen grape juice can be used if wild grapes are not available.

Ingredients
2 cups (500 mL) wild grape juice*
1 tsp (5 mL) cloves
2 cinnamon sticks
peel of 1 orange, grated
sugar
brandy (optional)

Method
1. Heat grape juice with spices and orange peel and add sugar to taste. Simmer for 15 minutes. Strain.
2. Add a dash of brandy if desired. Serve hot.

*Dilute juice with water if too strong.

Herbal Teas

The therapeutic virtues of herbs and plants are well documented and much talked about nowadays. Although I'd rather take a pill to cure a headache than drink half a gallon of wintergreen tea, medicinal herbs and plants do work if used as preventive medicine or over a long period of time.

My neighbor's mother-in-law is a tiny 74-year-old woman who raised seven children on a Prairie farm. The kids are all grown up now and left home long ago, but Mrs. L. still works from morning till night, baking bread, making jams, quilting, knitting, gardening, and babysitting her grandchildren. She attributes her unending energy to stinging nettle tea, which she brews from young shoots collected in the spring and dried. Her knowledge of herbs is extensive and her many herb mixes and ointments are in great demand among her friends.

I have tried her nettle tea, drinking one cup every morning for two weeks in the spring, and it did, indeed, give me a boost.

Yarrow

Yarrow
Achillea millefolium

It is said that Achilles, the Greek hero, used yarrow to treat the wounds of his soldiers, hence the name of the genus, *Achillea.* The name yarrow is a corruption of the Anglo-Saxon name for the plant, gearwe. Yarrow tea made with young leaves and budding flowers is astringent, tonic and stimulating, and is a good remedy for colds. A yarrow decoction can be used to clean wounds.

Once I was stung in two places at the same time by wasps. I thought "Great! Here is an opportunity to do a little test." On one sting, I applied commercial ointment. On the other, I spread a poultice made with fresh, young yarrow leaves crushed and mixed with water. One hour later, the pain and swelling was gone from the yarrow-treated wound while I still could feel the other, on which I promptly applied the natural medicine.

Labrador tea
Ledum groenlandicum

This low-growing northern shrub has leathery leaves with rolled margins and white or rusty fuzz underneath. The plant grows in peaty soils, bogs and alpine areas. Its leaves are tonic and pectoral, useful in treating coughs and irritation of the chest. The decoction is mildly narcotic and was used by Native women during childbirth.

Oxeye daisy
Chrysanthemum leucanthemum

This old-world perennial is found throughout North America. Tea made with fresh or dried flowers has medicinal properties similar to chamomile's and is antispasmodic, diuretic and tonic. Pick flowers when they are just open before bugs have a field day with them.

Conifer shoots

Young shoots from the branches of conifers, picked in spring when pale green and tender, produce a tea with woody flavors. Digestive and antiseptic, evergreen tea is recommended for colds, sore throats and liver disorders.

Most evergreen shoots can be used, but be sure not to pick Canada yew (*Taxus canadensis*), which is highly toxic. This yew is a low, straggling shrub with flat, pointed needles, green on both sides, and bearing red berries.

Conifer shoots make aromatic candies, best served after a rich meal to help digestion. To make them, in a heavy saucepan combine 1/3 cup (80 mL) sugar and 1/4 cup (60 mL) water. Bring to a boil. Add 12 conifer shoots and cook over medium heat until shoots are glazed with golden caramel.

Remove with tongs and dry on wax paper. Keep for up to 3 months in sealed container in a dry place.

Mint
Mentha

Rich in vitamins A and C, mint tea is digestive, stimulant, antiseptic and tonic. Drink it hot or cold for relief of flatulence, nausea and vomiting. People suffering from heart ailments should avoid mint because of its stimulating effect.

Stinging nettle
Urtica spp.

Like yarrow, stinging nettle is one of the most useful and versatile wild plants. The leaves can be dried to make tea. Pour hot, but not boiling, water over the leaves and infuse for 5 minutes. As a cleansing treatment, drink a small glass in the morning for a period of two weeks in spring and fall.

Remember, always wear gloves and long sleeves when picking stinging nettle. Tie the branches in a bunch and dry in a dark place.

Conifer shoots

Stinging nettle

Raspberry and Blackberry
Rubus spp.

Tea made with fresh or dried raspberry and blackberry leaves is astringent, depurative, diuretic and tonic. Pick leaves before flowers appear in the spring, or in the fall.

Wintergreen
Gaultheria procumbens

An important element in the pharmacopeia of Native peoples, wintergreen contains salicylate, a substance similar to ASA (aspirin) and having the same properties. To achieve the same effect as aspirin, however, you need to drink a gallon of wintergreen tea. Wintergreen essence is widely used to flavor toothpastes, mouthwashes and liniments, as well as to give scent to potpourris.

Wintergreen grows in hilly woodlands throughout central and eastern North America. It is a shrubby, creeping plant, seldom rising more than 4 inches (10 cm) off the ground. The erect, wiry stems hold a few oval-shaped leaves. The tiny, waxy, bell-shaped white flowers develop into bright red berries.

The leaves of wintergreen are evergreen and can be gathered all year. But when dried, young, tender, spring leaves keep their fragrance better than more mature leaves. Berries have the same spicy flavor as the leaves and are delicious eaten fresh.

Wintergreen

Coureur de Bois Tea

Ingredients

1/2 cup (125 mL) Labrador tea leaves
1/2 cup (125 mL) wintergreen leaves
1/4 cup (60 mL) conifer shoots

Method

1. Chop leaves or crumble them if dried. Mix thoroughly and keep in a tightly sealed glass jar in the dark.
2. Use 1 teaspoon (5 mL) for each cup (250 mL) of hot water. Infuse 5 minutes.

Magic Potion

Rich in minerals and vitamins, this herbal tea is excellent as a spring cleansing treatment.

Ingredients

yarrow leaves
stinging nettle leaves

Method

1. Pour hot, but not boiling, water over fresh or dried leaves.
2. Infuse 5 minutes.

Jellies and Butters

Jellies are easy to make. The only require-

ment for success is the right "jelly point",

which is difficult to measure even with a

candy thermometer as it depends a lot on

the pectin content of the fruit. Jelly point is

220˚F (105˚C). The best way to test the jelly

is by placing some on a saucer to see what

the consistency is like when it cools a bit.

(Instructions for making fruit juices are on page 17.)

Apple-Sherry Jelly

Makes four 16-ounce (500 mL) jars

Ingredients

3 cups (750 mL) apple juice
1 cup (250 mL) sherry
6 cups (1.5 L) sugar
1 pouch (3 oz/85 mL) liquid pectin (see below)

Method

1. Combine apple juice, sherry and sugar in a large heavy saucepan. Bring slowly to a boil, stirring frequently to dissolve sugar.
2. Add pectin and boil for 1 minute, stirring constantly.
3. Remove from heat. Skim off any foam that has formed and let stand 5 minutes. Ladle into hot jars, clean rims and seal with hot lids.

Liquid pectin usually comes in a pouch and is sold in boxes of two.

Port and Wild Grape Jelly

Makes four 16-ounce (500 mL) jars

Ingredients

3 cups (750 mL) wild grape juice
1 cup (250 mL) ruby port
juice of 1/2 lemon
6 cups (1.5 L) sugar
1 pouch (3 oz/85 mL) liquid pectin

Method

1. Combine grape juice, port, lemon juice and sugar.
2. Follow instructions for Apple-Sherry Jelly (above).

Apple and Mint Jelly

Makes three 16-ounce (500 mL) jars

Ingredients

1 cup (250 mL) mint leaves
4 cups (1 L) wild apple juice
4 cups (1 L) sugar

Method

1. Place mint leaves in cheesecloth and tie.
2. Combine all ingredients in a large heavy saucepan. Bring slowly to a boil, stirring till the sugar is dissolved. Boil until a candy thermometer reaches the jelly point (220°F/105°C). Remove bag of mint and skim off any foam that has formed.
3. Ladle into hot sterilized jars. Seal.

Serve with hot scones.

Apple Butter

Makes four 16-ounce (500 mL) jars

Ingredients

7 cups (1.75 L) apple pulp or compote
3 cups (750 mL) sugar
2 tsp (10 mL) cinnamon
1 tsp (5 mL) ground cloves

Method

1. Combine all ingredients in a heavy saucepan. Heat slowly, stirring constantly to prevent bottom from burning, and simmer until desired consistency is reached.
2. To check consistency, drop a teaspoonful of apple butter on a saucer and cool in the fridge for a couple of minutes. Butter should be firm and not runny.
3. Ladle into hot sterilized jars and seal.

Vinegars

Yarrow Vinegar

Makes 4 cups (1 L)

Ingredients

4 cups (1 L) apple cider vinegar
1 cup (250 mL) yarrow leaves

Method

1. Pick young tender leaves. Macerate in vinegar for 3 weeks in the sun. Strain and bottle.

2. Use to season dandelion salad (see page 49) or mesclun (see page 45).

Raspberry Vinegar

Makes 6 cups (1.5 L)

Ingredients

6 cups (1.5 L) apple cider vinegar
2 cups (500 mL) raspberries

Method

1. Place raspberries in a glass jar. Cover with vinegar and place in the sun for 3 weeks.
2. Strain and bottle.

Veal Liver with Raspberry Vinegar Sauce: Sauté liver in butter. Deglaze pan with raspberry vinegar, reduce liquid a couple of minutes over high heat. Pour over liver and serve.

Mint Vinegar

Makes 6 cups (1.5 L)

Ingredients

6 cups (1.5 L) apple cider vinegar
10 mint sprigs

Method

1. Place vinegar and mint in a glass jar or bottle and macerate for 3 weeks in the sun.
2. Strain and bottle.

This vinegar makes a refreshing drink. Mix 1 tablespoon (15 mL) into a large glass of chilled water.

Lamb Chops with Mint Vinegar: Fry chops in butter, 2 minutes on each side. Remove from pan and keep warm. Deglaze pan with mint vinegar. Reduce over high heat. Pour sauce over chops and serve.